COMPANION P|

THE ULTIMATE BEGINNER'S GUIDE TO COMPANION GARDENING; A CHEMICAL FREE METHOD TO GROW ORGANIC AND HEALTHY VEGETABLES AT HOME DETERRING PESTS AND INCREASING YIELD.

BY EDWARD GREEN

© **Copyright 2019 - All rights reserved.**

The content contained within this book may not be reproduced, duplicated or transmitted without direct written permission from the author or the publisher.

Under no circumstances will any blame or legal responsibility be held against the publisher, or author, for any damages, reparation, or monetary loss due to the information contained within this book. Either directly or indirectly.

Legal Notice:

This book is copyright protected. This book is only for personal use. You cannot amend, distribute, sell, use, quote or paraphrase any part, or the content within this book, without the consent of the author or publisher.

Disclaimer Notice:

Please note the information contained within this document is for educational and entertainment purposes only. All effort has been executed to present accurate, up to date, and reliable, complete information. No warranties of any kind are declared or implied. Readers acknowledge that the author is not engaging in the rendering of legal, financial, medical or professional advice. The content within this book has been derived from various sources. Please consult a licensed professional before attempting any techniques outlined in this book.

By reading this document, the reader agrees that under no circumstances is the author responsible for any losses, direct or indirect, which are incurred as a result of the use of information contained within this document, including, but not limited to, — errors, omissions, or inaccuracies.

Table of Contents

Introduction 1

Chapter 1. What is Companion Gardening? 3

Chapter 2. Companion Gardening Methods 10

Chapter 3. Allelopathy 14

Chapter 4. Insects: The Good Ones and the Bad Ones 21

Chapter 5. Full Sun or Partial Shade Garden (Lighting) 40

Chapter 6. Planning Your Garden 44

Chapter 7. Companion Plants 58

Chapter 8. Soil Improvement 70

Chapter 9. Common Mistakes of Companion Planting 81

Chapter 10. Perfect Combination 91

Chapter 11. The Importance of Compost for Soil Quality 101

Chapter 12. Good and Bad Companion 113

Chapter 13. Make Your Special Mix for Infilling Compost............... 123

Chapter 14. How to Grow Healthy Organic Herbs 130

Conclusion 136

Introduction

A successful garden is based on maximizing use of space, increasing crop productivity, pollination and pest control. Companion planting, meaning planting different crops in proximity, is beneficial for all of these things and more.

In the past few years, companion planting is receiving a lot of attention from the scientific community because it can help reduce the need for harmful chemicals in farming. Home gardeners are re-discovering this information and using it to their benefit.

This book is made to teach you how to start Companion Planting and grow a successful garden full of healthy vegetables, fruits and herbs that all benefit from each other to grow better.

In order to start, keep in consideration the following:

Seasonality is a basic rule of thumb when considering companion planting: for example, radishes and greens grow well together, as they both like cold temperatures and well-drained soil; tomatoes and squash grow well together, as they both like lots of suns and do well in the heat, while peppers also thrive at this time of year and provide some natural pest repellent.

Space can also be a common-sense product of companion planting wisdom: planting lower growing herbs such as tarragon, oregano, and rosemary in between tomato plants give vines room to spread while also providing pest protection. Also, sequential planting is another sub-category of companion planting—planting continuously throughout the year—has the added benefit of discouraging weed growth.

These are merely a handful of examples of the vast reserve of material concerning the benefits and techniques of companion planting. Farmers Almanacs, farmers' markets, cooperative extension services are all excellent places to get further advice on how to set up your garden for maximum success.

What is Companion Gardening?

What is Companion Gardening and the Science behind It

Companion gardening is simply a form of Polyculture. When used intelligently along with gardening techniques such as Raised Bed Gardening or Container Gardening, for instance, then it is the method of sharing the mutual benefits of the individual plants, is capable of producing fantastic results. Companion planting is likened to putting together the perfect partnership, creating results in respect of more abundant, healthier crops that the individual plants could not produce.

The fact is that, just like we homo-sapiens, plants need good companions to thrive and flourish in their environment. Unlike us, however, is rooted to the spot, they cannot choose their friends – we have to choose friends or companions for them! We take into account the strong points and needs of the individual plants and then put them together – in fact, the gardener takes on the role of match-maker!

Will I bet you never considered running a dating agency for vegetables before this – did you? Joking apart; the fact is that if the plants thrive – alongside the ideal companions that you have provided - then the harvest is bountiful – and everyone is happy.

Companion planting is nothing new; and is reasonably well documented. The Chinese, for instance, have been using this method to protect and promote their rice crops for over 1,000 years.

By planting the mosquito fern as a companion for their rice crops, that hosts a special CYANOBACTERIUM that fixes nitrogen from the atmosphere. It also helps to block out the light so that competing weeds cannot prosper, the rice being planted when it is tall enough to stick above the fern.

The native Indians of North America are widely accredited for pioneering the 'Three Sisters' technique of planting corn, beans and squash together. The corn would act as a trellis for the beans, which in turn laid down nitrogen that benefited the corn and the squash. Sunflowers could also be grown, usually a short distance away from the three sisters to act help draw away aphids.

Companion planting, although ancient in origin, has grown up alongside the whole Organic Farming movement. With the emphasis on healthier foods, organically grown, this holistic approach to growing vegetables has taken on whole new importance for the modern, environmentally aware grower.

What are the Benefits of Companion Gardening

Many reasons can be cited to promote the idea of companion planting, from environmental to personal. Here are just five of the most important reasons:

1. Environmental

Protecting the environment is a hugely important issue these days and rightly so. If more people got themselves involved with the principles behind organic and companion gardening, then we would not be polluting both our bodies and the land, with chemical fertilizers or poisonous insecticides to the extent that we are.

It does not just involve ourselves but has ramifications for generations to come.

Millions of tons of waste going into landfills every year, which in fact could easily be recycled – to our benefit! Composting is a part of growing your vegetables, and becoming more environmentally aware is one way to help balance its wastage.

It can be correctly stated that companion planting, when done in concert with other organic growing methods, is good for our bodies and good for the environment – a win-win situation.

2. Productivity

The main principle behind companion planting is the fact that when individual plants are grown together, then they benefit from one another or at least the different plants can be grown together because they have different needs. It means that they are not competing for the same nutrients or even atmospheric conditions.

With It being the case, then it also means that you can have a higher volume of plants in the same growing area, as they can be grown closer together without it being detrimental in any way –, if done correctly, they will benefit from It closeness.

3. Easy maintenance:

The reason that companion planting generally means easier maintenance is that it may not at first be recognized. However, the fact is that if the plants are appropriately chosen, it means that they are planted closer together, meaning less of an area to cover when maintaining or harvesting your vegetables.

It is especially relevant in a raised bed situation, where the area you have to cover is limited to the confines of the raised bed.

In It situation you have a 'double score' so to speak; as a raised bed garden is not so prone to weeds anyway, It coupled with correct companion planting, where the sunshine and nutrients are denied to weeds; leads to a situation where you can maximize your efforts and get better results.

4. Natural insect control:

One of the big pluses for the companion planter is the fact that fewer insect problems occur if the plants accompanying their neighbors are correctly chosen. For instance, if onions or leeks are planted alongside carrots, then problems with the dreaded carrot fly are less of an issue as the smell of the onions detracts the fly from the carrots.

Marigolds planted alongside your tomatoes will attract hoverflies, which will protect them against aphids.

More examples to follow!

5. Less need for fertilizer

Again, if done correctly using organic methods of growing your vegetables, then there will be little if any need for fertilizer.

The reason is two-fold. Firstly good organic compost in your growing area means that fertilizer should not be needed unless you are perhaps aiming to grow 'super crops.'

Secondly, if the plants are appropriately rotated, then the needs of one plant may be supplied by the waste or productivity of another. For instance, legumes like peas and beans can draw nitrogen from the atmosphere and deposit it into the ground. It benefits a multitude of other plants that flourish in nitrogen-rich soil.

Companion Gardening Methods

Companion gardening has been practiced in many different ways that vary from place to place. While many people know the term companion gardening, there are obscure lines that have in the recent past arisen between the practice and other forms of smart gardening. In short, it may be possible that so many people are practicing organic gardening, only that they refer to it with a different word and are oblivious of the fact that they are doing it. Below are the significant methods of companion gardening.

1. Square foot Gardening

Square foot gardening is a practice that attempts to protect plants from traditional gardening woes by planting them on particular soil as well as close to each other. Crops are planted on hybrid soil, which is a mixture of compost, peat and vermiculite. The soil has all the nutrients that re needed for the crops to thrive. After this, the soil is placed in an isolated environment where it does not mix with other soils and crops planted on each square foot of the garden. To create a picture of what the ideal farm must be, the gardener divides the top of the box with strips that mark out boxes that are equal in size. In each square foot, the farmer will plant a different crop, thus effectively growing more than ten types of crops in a single sixteen square meter space. It method generally achieves better results than traditional companion cropping as the crops are grown close together, and they are thus able to interact and form a rigid front against pests and deceases.

2. Forest Garden

Forest gardening refers to creating a plant ecosystem from scratch. It is done by planting a forest and increasingly planting smaller crops between the rows. They planted crops also form a shade or host to an additional row, which leads to a very vast ecosystem. Its system has up to seven levels of growth, and plants can be planted of up to 14 varieties, alternating between plants of different varieties in the rows. Plants are grown in woodlands where they cover each other and help each other grow and also resist pests and deceases. In elephant infested woodlands, for instance, crops may be protected by simply adding an extra row of pepper in the garden. It will keep the jumbos off the farm. It may also help keep primates off the gardens too. Forest gardening opens up a new way of intercropping or simply companion cropping as the crops will help each other in different stages of growth.

3. Organic Gardening

It is the most common type of companion gardening. Organic gardening generally refers to a type of gardening where the farmer will avoid the use of inorganic materials and inputs in growing the garden. The basic idea of this is that the farmer will use companion crops to fight off each other's pests as well as discourage disease spread. Organic gardening emphasizes natural farm inputs as opposed to extreme use of chemicals, which is encouraging companion crops to be substituted for chemicals. It also encourages farmers to have some real natural barriers to pests and disease, some of which are other crops. In the end, there is a myriad of names that draw their concept from companion gardening and will thus be most likely to be called by their other names. However, the idea behind all this is almost always companion gardening. Thus, organic gardening is simply a fancy and advanced form of companion gardening.

4. Spatial Interaction

Spatial interactions involve placing individual plants that affect other plants in the same vicinity. These interactions can be chemical, benefiting the growth of the other plant, or they could attract beneficial insects to your garden.

5. Nurse Cropping

Methods of nurse cropping include the Seven Layer System, where some larger plants shield the smaller ones.

6. Three Sisters Method

It is the method with the planting of three different veggies together with each plant benefitting the others. Corn, beans and squash are the typical combinations used in the Three Sisters Method, but there are others as well.

7. Container Gardens

Container gardens consist of simple plastic five-gallon buckets with or without an automated watering system built-in. These container gardens minimize weeds; help you eliminate problems with poor soil with the added benefit of being able to rearrange individual plants after they begin growing.

8. Layer System

The seven-layer system utilizes the size and type of plants in what is called a 'forest garden.' These plants and trees grow together, with each benefiting the others.

- The Canopy Layer: is made up of large fruit or nut trees (not walnut trees). These trees provide the shade or canopy that protects the sixth layer plants (the ground cover) from too much sun exposure and excess winds. These trees also provide support

for the seventh layer of plants, which are the climbers or vine plants.
- Low Tree Layer: includes the dwarf fruit trees that sit under the canopy of the more giant trees.
- Shrub Layer: consists of the bushes that grow berries and other types of fruits. These are protected by both the more giant trees and the low tree layer.
- Herbaceous Layer: are the beets or herbs that grow in the shade of the hedge.
- RHIZOSPHERE Layer: Root vegetables like carrots, potatoes and more are the RHIZOSPHERE Layer. They benefit from the shade and the water that the more giant trees bring up from the water table.
- Soil Surface: These are the ground cover in the first layer. These include strawberries. The ground cover prevents weeds from infiltrating the ecosystem and provides yet another beneficial fruit in your garden.
- Vertical Layer: Also, in the first layer, the Vertical Layer includes cucumbers, grapes and other vine fruits and vegetables.

Allelopathy

ALLELOPATHY is best described as chemical warfare between plants. One plant can suppress another and to take advantage of that situation. The word is derived from two Ancient Greek words, 'ALLELON,' meaning each other and 'pathos' which means to suffer.

Therefore, ALLELOPATHIC plants deliberately create adverse growing conditions that stunt and kill off neighboring plants. It can be by reducing germination rates or seedling growth or just plain killing off competing plants. Used wisely, ALLELOPATHIC plants can be a great alternative to chemicals!

Plants compete for resources such as space, water, nutrition, and sunlight. Some compete by snowballing; others spread out wide or send down deep roots. Other plants have developed analytic tools for getting the resources they require to flourish.

ALLELOPATHIC plants release compounds from the roots into the soil, which then suppress or kill their neighbors as they are sucked up through their root systems. These harmful chemicals are unsurprising, known as ALLELOCHEMICALS. Some of these chemicals can go as far as changing the level of chlorophyll production, which can then slow down or even stop photosynthesis, which leads to the death of the plant.

A lot of ALLELOPATHIC plants release chemicals in gas form from small pores in their leaves. As their neighbors absorb these gasses, they are either suppressed or killed.

Some ALLELOPATHIC plants deal with the competition when their leaves fall to the ground. The leaves decompose and release chemicals that then inhibit nearby plants.

There are a lot of different plants that have ALLELOPATHIC tendencies, but it isn't particularly common. Sometimes, however, you can very quickly plant an ALLELOPATHIC plant near one of its victims without realizing it and wonder why some of your plants struggle to grow.

The black walnut tree is probably the master of chemical warfare in the plant kingdom. Its leaves, roots, nut hulls and buds have ALLELOPATHIC properties, and it also secretes JUGLONE into the soil, which inhibits respiration in many plants. The black walnut guards its resources so jealously that virtually nothing will grow near to one. Many a gardener has rejoiced at the black walnut tree in their garden until they realized that nothing would grow near it.

ALLELOPATHIC characteristics can be found in any part of a plant, whether it is the root, bark, flowers, seeds, fruits, leaves, or pollen. It varies from plant to plant, though the majority of plants store their ALLELOPATHIC chemicals in their leaves.

Some common plants that are known to have ALLELOPATHIC properties include:

- English laurel

- Elderberry

- Bearberry

- Rhododendron

- Junipers, which hamper the growth of grasses

- Perennial rye hampers the growth of apple trees

- Sugar maple hampers the growth of yellow birch and white spruce

If you think about where you see these plants growing, you will see very little growing underneath or near them.

There is a lot of research underway into ALLELOPATHIC plants, and the list of plants is regularly being updated. These plants are exciting to farmers for their properties, which could well find their way into genetically modified seeds.

The advantage of ALLELOCHEMICALS is that they can produce natural herbicides and pesticides. Planting the right plants together as companions will keep down certain weeds, which can reduce reliance on chemical herbicides. When pairings are chosen well, the ALLELOPATHIC plant will even have a positive effect on your chosen vegetable crop.

ALLELOPATHIC research is still very much in its infancy as researchers try to understand its interaction between plants. Some research papers published, and you can use this effect to your benefit in your garden. If you have established plants already present in your garden and are struggling to grow anything else, it may be that one of these plants has ALLELOPATHIC properties.

Be aware that ALLELOCHEMICALS can build up in the soil, and it can take several years for the levels of these chemicals to drop so that other plants will grow. Years ago, I removed an English laurel tree from my garden as it was too large. Underneath was bare soil. Nothing had grown there, but when I dug over the soil and added manure, everything I planted died. It was several years and a lot of fertilizer and compost before anything would grow in that area again. If you have to remove ALLELOPATHIC plants, then you may want to consider removing 12-18 inches of soil and replacing it if you struggle to get anything to grow in that space.

Insects: The Good Ones and the Bad Ones

Beneficial Insects for Your Garden

The good news is that insect pests are far outnumbered by insect allies in our gardens and yards. Without bees, no flower will be pollinated, and in this regard, many kinds of moths and flies make their contribution. Many beneficial insects prey on pest insects, and parasitic insects will lay their eggs right inside the pest insects. When the larvae hatch, they usually kill or at least weaken their hosts. Other ally insects like flies and dung beetles assist in the breaking down of decaying matter in the garden and so help to build good fertile soil. Therefore, I will name the fourteen most beneficial insects to have around and how you can lure them to your garden and convince them to make it their new home.

- **Wasps and Bees**

Bees

There is a good reason why people in agricultural circles refer to honeybees as their 'spark plugs.' They are essential for pollinating crops. However, they are not the only pollinators around; wild bees make their contribution as well and act as agents of pest control on top of it all. Pollen and nectar are used by all bees to feed on; they also gather it for their nests. It is the main distinction between them and hornets and wasps. They fly from one flower to another in their quest for food and, in the process, distribute pollen grains amongst the different flowers they visit, pollinating blooms as they go along.

It has not yet been determined what the cause of its disorder is, but what we know is that the worker bees just suddenly start to die, leaving their queen bee, nursing bees and as yet unborn brood without the necessary support. Eventually, the whole hive collapses. Speculation is rife; maybe it is caused by parasites or diseases, maybe the damage done by chemical pesticides to their nervous and immune systems.

Luckily our tiny little 'sweet bees,' bumblebees and other natives are still active and doing their bit to pollinate garden plants and crops. So, how can you encourage these native bees? Plant enough flowers to last the bees as long as possible. Allow some bare, open ground for them where they can tunnel and build their nests. Also, make sure they have access to water in a shallow container.

Yellow Jackets

Hornets and yellow jackets are feared by most people, but they have an essential role to play as pest predators. Diving into foliage, they target caterpillars, flies and larvae, which they feed to their offspring. So, unless someone in your family is allergic to their stings or they are living in an area frequented by pets and people, do not destroy their nests.

Beetles

Ground Beetles

Ground beetles are blue-black, swift-footed, and hideaway under boards and stone during the daylight hours. Come to the darkness of night, and they emerge to feed on slug and snail eggs, cutworms and root maggots. They even climb trees in search of tent caterpillars and armyworms. Large populations can live in gardens underneath the stone pathways, semi-permanent mulched vegetable or flower beds or the undisturbed groundcovers of orchards.

Lady Beetles

Everyone knows lady beetles with their hard, shiny bodies. There are around three thousand species in total, and they prey on soft, small pests like spider mites, MEARLYBUGS and aphids. I have to mention that not all the species are right for your garden, for example, the Mexican bean beetle. The larvae, as well as the adult beetles, will feed on pests. The larvae resemble tiny miniature alligators with their tapered bodies and branching spines. You can buy convergent ladybugs at some garden centers. They overwinter in mass where they are collected. But it is not easy to keep them in your garden unless you have a greenhouse.

Rove Beetles

Rove beetles have elongated bodies with stubby, short wings, resembling earwigs' pinchers. They are active decomposers and will work away at plant material and manure. Others prey on root maggots.

Flies

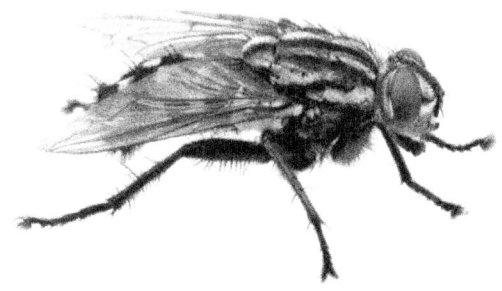

The TACHINID Fly

These flies are dark gray, bristly and large and lay their larvae or eggs on stinkbugs, corn borers, caterpillars and cutworms amongst other pests. They are quite effective against the outbreaks of armyworm and tent caterpillar.

The SYRPHID Fly

These flies are also called hover or flower flies. They are easily recognizable by their black and white or yellow stripes. Still, They are also often mistakenly identified as yellow jackets or even bees. After laying their eggs inside aphids, their larvae devour the aphids. The larvae are translucent, unattractive gray maggots and resemble small slugs, so do not be misled by their appearance.

Aphid Midges

The larva of this fly is a tiny orange maggot and will feed voraciously on aphids. They can be purchased at commercial insectaries. Release them into your greenhouse, and you will see the positive effects very soon.

Insects That Don't Benefit the Garden and How to Get Rid of Them Naturally

Bad Insects

While the perfect garden would only attract beneficial insects that would prey on anything and everything that dared step foot into the garden, that's rarely the case. Most gardens contain a wide variety of insects, both good and bad.

Let's take a closer look at some of the more common pests found in gardens across the country. If you're lucky, you won't have to deal with more than one or two of these insects at once.

Aphids

Aphids, also known as plant lice, can have up to 12 live babies per day. Within the first week, one aphid can have 84 babies. Within a week, those aphids are ready to start having babies of their own. The 84 babies will start adding 12 babies apiece per day, which is more than 1,000 aphids being added daily. Once they start having babies, the numbers jump even more dramatically. Within a month, millions of aphids will be infesting the garden. Of course, this simple scenario assumes no aphids die and that each of the aphids has exactly 12 babies per day, but you get the point.

Luckily, you have some options when it comes to control aphids. You can plant caraway, chamomile, dandelions, buckwheat and tansy to attract insects that prey on them. Ladybugs, green lacewings, praying mantises, and minute pirate bugs will all make a meal of aphids. Nasturtiums can be used as a trap crop for aphids.

Additionally, you can use the following plants to repel aphids

- Basil.
- Catnip.
- Chives.
- Clover.
- Coriander.
- Dill.
- Eucalyptus.
- Fennel.
- Garlic.
- Onions.

- Nettles.

- Peppermint.

- Radishes.

Caterpillars

To keep caterpillars at bay, add plants to your garden that draw in parasitic wasps, praying mantises and green lacewings. Another option is to hang a bird feeder to call in birds that'll come for the bird food and supplement their meals with any caterpillars that cross their paths. When you see a caterpillar, handpick it and move it far from your garden.

The following plants can be planted in a garden to repel caterpillars:

• Lavender.

• Peppermint.

• Sage.

Colorado potato beetle

The Colorado potato beetle looks like a yellowish-orange ladybug with stripes instead of dots. While ladybugs are a preferred predator in the garden and will eat Colorado potato beetles, these pests will quickly defoliate peppers, potatoes, eggplant and tomatoes. In addition to ladybugs, nematodes are beneficial to have around when potato beetles are present.

Some sources indicate the Colorado potato beetle doesn't like to walk over coarse mulch. Adding a layer of straw mulch around your plants may prevent the beetle from making it to your plants.

The following plants will repel Colorado potato beetles:

- Catnip.

- Chives.

- Coriander.

- Eucalyptus.

- Garlic.

- Green beans.

- Marigolds.

- Nasturtiums.

- Peas.

Flea Beetles

These tiny little pests are found across the entirety of North America. They chew small, round holes in the leaves of most vegetables and will jump around nervously when disturbed. Flea beetles prefer dry soil to lay their eggs in, so keep your soil damp to make your garden less attractive. Nematodes can be added to the soil to make short work of any larvae that do hatch.

The following plants will repel flea beetles:

- Catnip.

- Peppermint.

- Rue.

- Thyme.

Mexican bean beetle

The Mexican bean beetle is a connoisseur of several varieties of beans. It has a bottomless pit for a stomach and will continue chewing on the leaves of a plant until it starts to die. These beetles roam the Western half of the United States, looking for bean crops to devastate.

The following plants are known to repel Mexican bean beetles

- Garlic.

- Marigolds.

- Rosemary.

Japanese Beetles

Japanese beetles are commonly found in the Eastern half of the United States. They are known to attack a variety of vegetables and flowers. They're a bluish-green color and feature rust-colored wing covers. They're pretty to look at, but the damage they can do to a crop is anything but pretty.

The following plants will deter Japanese beetles:

- Catnip.

- Chives.

- Chrysanthemums.

- Garlic.

- Marigolds.

- Onions.

- Rue.

Scales

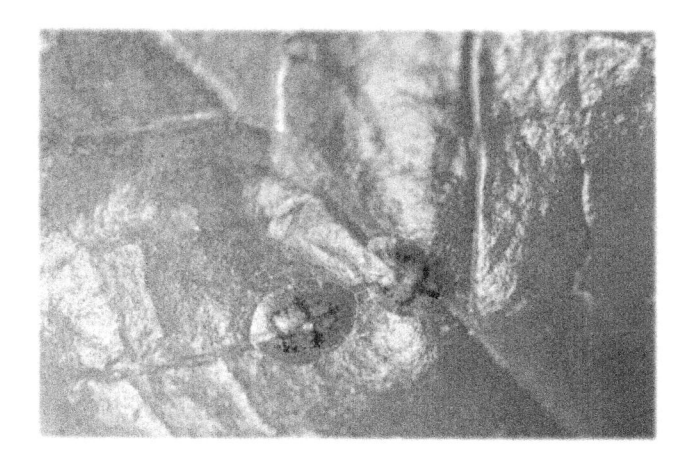

Scales are aptly named because, at a glance, they look like small scales attached to a plant. They're destructive little creatures that will suck sap from plants during every stage of their life cycle. When you notice scales on your plants, prune them back to get rid of the affected areas or scrub them off the branches.

There are no plants that are known to deter scales, so you'll have to rely on predatory insects to get the job done. Ladybugs, praying mantises, and green lacewings will all dine on scales, so plants that attract them may help.

Tomato FRUITWORMS (Corn Earworms)

Tomato FRUITWORMS, also known as corn earworms, cotton bollworms and geranium budworms, are found in gardens throughout North America. These worms are known by several names, usually indicative of the type of plant they're attacking. They've been known to dine on cotton, beans, peas, peppers, tomatoes, corn, geraniums, potatoes and squash.

The adults are small moths that lay eggs on the bottoms of leaves. The larvae feed on the leaves as they grow. If they're attacking a corn crop, they'll move into the husks as the corn matures and will eventually begin to feed on the silk and the corn kernels at the ends of the ears.

Geraniums and thyme are known to deter the tomato FRUITWORMS.

Tomato Hornworm

This giant caterpillar is found in gardens throughout the United States, usually munching on the leaves of eggplant, peppers, potatoes and tomatoes. They develop into giant moths that have a wingspan of up to 5".

The following plants will repel tomato hornworms:

- Borage

- Dill
- Thyme

Full Sun or Partial Shade Garden (Lighting)

One of the most significant decisions you're going to have to make is whether you're going to grow a full sun or a partial shade garden. If you're limited on space, It decision may have already been made for you, and you're going to have to work with what you've got. The amount of sun and shade an area gets is one of the major determining factors of the types of plants that can be grown there.

Most fruits and vegetables prefer full sun, so if you're looking to grow a produce garden, that's the way to go.

That isn't to say they all prefer sitting in the middle of a desert baking in hot sunlight. Full sun is defined as at least 6 hours of sunlight per day, while some plants need as many as 8 to 10 hours per day to thrive. Trying to grow plants that require full sun in an area that gets less exposure to the sun than this will be an exercise in frustration. The plants may grow, but yields will be reduced, and they'll be more susceptible to attack from pests and disease.

Partial shade or partial sun implies a plant needs less sunlight and can get by on 3 to 6 hours of sunlight per day. These plants do best when they're shaded from the sun in the afternoon when it's at its peak. Placing a plant that prefers partial shade or partial sun in an area that gets full sunlight can scorch the plant when temperatures start to climb, causing it to wilt or even die.

Full shade means relatively little sunlight. There may be a small handful of plants you can grow in full shade, but without much light, you're going to be very limited. If you want to plant fruit and vegetables, you're going to have to find another spot.

Most vegetables, fruits and herbs prefer full sunlight. If you have a garden that only gets partial sunlight, you're going to have to select plants that can be grown with only partial sunlight. There isn't a whole lot you can do to increase the amount of sunlight an area gets short of chopping down trees, moving mountains or tearing down buildings. Reflective mulches can be used to reflect sunlight up to plants, but the effect is minimal.

Lettuce, spinach, radishes and some varieties of strawberries are well-suited to partially-shaded garden areas. Other crops like peas and potatoes will grow in partial shade, but yields will be reduced. To be clear, these plants will still need sunlight to grow—they just don't need as much as some of the needier plants.

Those looking to grow plants that require partial shade in a full sun location have a handful of options at their disposal. For one, you can build a structure that provides shade during certain times of the day. It's best to build a shade that provides relief from the afternoon sun, as opposed to one that provides shade in the morning. Afternoon sunlight is hotter and more likely to damage plants than morning sunlight. Another option is to set up latticework through which the sun can shine. Your plants will get sunlight throughout the day, but won't be exposed to the constant heat of the sun. Some plants will do better than others with It technique, so experiment to find out what works best.

You may be wondering what all this has to do with companion planting. Some plants grow tall or have large leaves that spread out that can be used to provide shade to smaller plants. The larger plants can be planted as companion plants to smaller plants that need partial shade. Corn, sunflowers, tomatoes and artichokes can all be planted to provide shade for smaller plants. Trellises plants like pole beans and grapes are also an excellent way to provide dappled sunlight, which is the light that's filtered through the leaves of the trellised plant.

These larger sun-loving plants can be planted to provide shade for plants like cabbage, broccoli and cauliflower that don't do well when temperatures start to climb as summer approaches. Smaller plants like carrots, cucumbers and lettuce can also benefit from being planted in the shade of a taller plant as long as the taller plants don't surround them and completely block out the sun.

Trees can be used to provide shade, but you have to be careful not to use a variety of tree that's going to grow to great heights and completely block sunlight from reaching your garden. If trees are already present and are providing too much shade, you may be able to top them or prune them back to ensure your garden gets ample sunlight.

Planning Your Garden

Before you start your companion garden, like any project that you intend to build successfully, you will need to draw up some plans. The plan for this type of garden may contain the following seven significant steps:

Make a List of the Vegetables You Need To Grow

Everything starts with a list. You must have a list of all the vegetables you will need for your family. Depending upon what type of garden you want to grow, you will have to determine the best options for the region in which you are residing. Each region has its seasonal vegetables, fruits, and herbs. You will need to plan so you can make the most of what you can grow naturally with the least amount of effort. In case you are looking for vegetables that do not typically grow in your region, you can always consider building a small greenhouse.

Identify the Best Companion Plants for Your Vegetables

Once you decide what vegetables you want to grow, the logical step is to find out what are the best companion plants for your garden. Do refer to Table No one shown earlier regarding the best matches between plants. While the list is not all-inclusive, it does give a good idea about how to go about pairing your favorite vegetable plants to ensure that you have an outstanding harvest.

To help you decide what companion plants to choose, take into account what type of beneficial pests, beneficial insects/ animals/ and micro-organisms your vegetables will usually attract in the region in which you live, then chose those plants that will help your garden the most. Seek the assistance of an expert in the first 1-2 years if you are not sure what to do. After some time, you will gain enough experience to make your own decisions.

Draw a Map of the Garden

Draw a map of your garden and annotate where you want your plants to be planted. It is imperative to have this map because you will have to rotate the places of the vegetables every year to ensure that the soil will remain fertile and rich enough to encourage the optimal growth of your favorite vegetables. For the best results, you would need to rotate the placement every year or at the most once every two years.

While drawing up the map of the garden, you should keep in mind that the taller plants should be positioned such that they should not overshadow the smaller plants. For a garden to grow well, each plant should have adequate (as per the need of the plant) access to sunshine, shade, and water.

Calculate the Sowing Date

Each plant has a particular sowing date. You will need to calculate the right time to plant the vegetables so you will not lose your harvest owing to unfavorable climatic conditions. To know the sowing date, you will need to subtract the growth period from the planting date. It is the date when you should sow seeds indoors, outdoors, or in a greenhouse to have the seedlings ready for transplant after the last frost. Table No two will help gather an idea about this exercise.

Here it is important to note that you should know which vegetable will grow well if seeds are sown directly in the garden soil and which seeds need to be "started" indoors or in a greenhouse for transplanting once the frost is gone. The last date of frost in your climatic region can be readily ascertained from an almanac

Calculating Sowing Date

Seed/Plant	Write in Sow Date	Growth Period # of Weeks	Safe Set-Out Date (Relative to Last Frost)
Beans*		8 to 10	
Beets*		8 to 10	2-3 weeks after
Broccoli		8 to 10	2 weeks before
Brussels Sprouts		16 to 19	3 weeks before
Cabbage		13 to 17	3 weeks before
Carrots*		8 to 10	1-2 weeks after
Cauliflower		8 to 10	2 weeks before
Collards		4 to 6	4 weeks before
Corn*		9 to 12	2 weeks after
Cucumber*		6 to 12	1-2 weeks after
Eggplant		14 to 20	3 weeks after
Lettuce		4 to 7	1-2 weeks after
Greens*		5 to 7	Soon as soil can be worked
Okra		4 to 6	2-4 weeks after
Onion*		8 to 10	2-3 weeks before
Parsley		8 to 10	2 weeks before
Peas*		8 to 10	4-6 weeks before
Peppers		8 to 10	2 weeks after
Potatoes*		10 to 20	2-3 weeks after
Pumpkin*		15 to 18	2-3 weeks after
Radish*		4	3-4 weeks before
Spinach*		6 to 7	3-6 weeks before
Winter Squash*		13 to 22	2 weeks after
Tomato		8 to 12	1 week after
Zucchini*		2 to 4	2 weeks after

Find the Seeds or Seedlings

Now that you have all the information necessary about your preferred vegetables and the companion plants, the step is to identify a right place from where you can purchase your seeds or seedlings. For vegetables that can be directly planted as seeds in the garden, buy from a reputed brand and read the instructions carefully before planting. For those vegetables which cannot thrive when planted as seeds, ensure that you either grow the seedlings to be ready at the right time or buy the ready-made seedlings.

Complete all of the preliminary work well in time for the planting season. Each vegetable will have a "right time" for sowing. Ensure that you know the right time and that you plan accordingly.

Planting Time

Plant your vegetables according to their appropriate time and the map you have drawn for your garden. Your garden should gradually change into the picture you had envisaged when you planned your garden. Add the necessary props where necessary, so the vegetable plants grow well.

For the planting to go well, you will need to have the soil ready, aired, tilled, watered, and fertilized, so when the seedling is planted, everything should work in favor of the plant.

Watering the Plants

It is crucial that the watering is planned well. Your garden needs to be designed in such a way that each plant will receive the amount of water it requires. You could use sprinklers that release the right amount of water at various locations in the garden. Be very careful not to flood the garden, for there is nothing more harmful to the plants than a soaking-wet soil. Not only does it develop root rot, but it also attracts many diseases and pests that love humidity and a dying plant.

Fertilizing the Garden

The garden needs to be fertilized well, so the plants draw their nutrients without depleting all the goodness existing in it. For the plants to grow well, they will need organic fertilizers, and these need to be added every year. Mulching often makes up for these needs, as is planting appropriate companion plants that pull nutrients for themselves and the plants in the vicinity.

For fertilizer, you need to learn to make your compost. Though composting material is available in garden supply stores as well as online stores, the best choice is to make your own. Add the fertilizer as and when it is needed. Do not overload the plant, or you will send the wrong signals to the pests in the vicinity.

How Do I actually Start Companion Planting?

Stage A. Crop Rotation

Treat crop rotation as the very first most essential element of companion planting.

Step 1: Choose plants that grow well in your particular location and soil type. If you have the time, resources and energy, you can alter your soil type. For beginner gardeners, it is better to find plants that suit their current garden soil. It is also a good idea to give some consideration to the following points

A. Ease of access to the site for tending, harvesting

B. Accessibility to gardening tools, compost heap, seating

C. Accessibility to water.

D. The size of beds, borders should be considered. You need to be able to get near to your plants from all sides.

E. Appropriate pathway materials. Bark mulch, paving, decking, gravel, grass are all options. Pathways should ideally be wide enough for a wheelbarrow. If space is limited, you could opt for a few more extensive paths and then have narrow paths coming off the broader paths.

F. Boundaries and windbreaks may also be needed. Fruit bushes could be an option.

Step 2: At this stage, you need to plan your garden layout.

For a reasonably accurate representation of your plans, you could draw your garden layout on graph paper. By using graph paper, you can let each square represent your preferred measurement, e.g., one square = one foot. You can also make allowances for permanent features such as trees or sheds by coloring in the appropriate amount of squares. Now transfer those dimensions represented on the graph paper into your garden. You can use stakes and twine, sand to mark out your scheme. You can also apply those measurements to a raised bed system.

At this stage, you will have decided on the basic layout of your garden and a crop rotation plan. Now it is time to consider adding some diversity to your plant selection.

Step 1: Different Cultivars

Plant different cultivars or go a step further and plant open-pollinated seeds. Open-pollinated seeds will produce plants that are not genetically the same as their parents. Its difference in the genetic make-up could save some of the plants from being destroyed by pest or disease attack.

Step 2: Flowers, Vegetables and Herbs

Add another layer of diversity by combining flowering plants and herbs with vegetable plants. You have several choices. You can create a permanent bed of perennials and bulbs, close to your vegetable beds. Color is always welcome, but you also create a home for beneficial insects.

To make better use of your available space, you could plant flowering plants or herbs between your vegetables. It is a winning combination.

Step 3: Soil Enrichment

It is common sense that plants derive nutrients from the soil, but it is also a fact that some plants give more to the soil than they take away.

Plants such as peas, beans, lentils, alfalfa, LUPINS, soybeans, mesquite and peanuts have an extraordinary relationship with a particular form of bacteria.

The plants named above belong to a group of plants known as legumes, and the particular bacteria are known as rhizobia.

This bacterium grows on the roots of legumes and can trap nitrogen gas and turn it into a form of nitrogen that can help the plant itself and other plants to grow. Some of the nitrogen is used by the plant itself, and when the plant dies, and its roots decompose, more nitrogen is released into the soil. Its nitrogen is then available to plants growing nearby. It does not end there, and if you remove the entire dead plant above and below soil level and then bury all of it back into the soil, it will release more nitrogen, which will boost the crop that is planted in that particular soil.

Many gardeners follow a crop rotation plan that involves growing legumes for two consecutive years and then on the third year growing non-legumes. There is usually sufficient nitrogen in the soil to produce good results.

The process of growing and digging-in legumes is generally referred to as green manure or cover cropping.

Step 4: Repel Bad Insects

We have made use of the ability of one plant to help another in this stage to deal with how one plant can attract/deter insects that may help/damage another plant.

Aromatic plants can release compound which hides the scent of another plant. Because the scent of plant one overpowers the scent off plant two, insects that could damage plant two are unaware of its existence, so they don't attack it. Examples of It process include growing

Summer Savory with your bush beans and growing tansy with your potatoes.

Aromatic plants will also deter insects just by the real pungency of their scent. Grow mint with cabbage, garlic with beans and potatoes and basil with tomatoes.

If you have space, you could dedicate an entire bed to these plants, or you could grow individual plants in the same bed as your vegetables.

Step 5: Decoy Plants

Certain insects love individual plants, so we make use of that attraction in two ways.

First, we grow these plants so that the insects are attracted to them. If they are concentrating on these plants, your primary plants are a lot safer.

Second, when we have most of these harmful insects in one location, i.e., on the attractive plant, we can remove that plant and thereby remove a lot of the insects. Just use a bag that is slightly bigger than the plant itself but big enough to drop it quickly over the plant. Drop the bag over the plant and quickly close the bag at the base of the plant. Place your hand at the base of the plant and pull. Now you can destroy/remove plants and insects at the same time.

Examples of decoy plants include growing Black Nightshade to attract Colorado Potato Beatles and growing Nasturtium to attract Aphids.

Step 6: Attract Good Insects

There are several types of insects that you want to attract to your garden. Creating a haven for these will provide you with these beneficial insects.

Provide food and shelter for them, and they will reward you with some great work.

Examples of It process include attracting insects such as spiders and lacewings that will eat cabbage caterpillars, cucumber beetles and aphids.

Stage C: Putting It All Together

Keep a logbook of your efforts during the year. You will need to mix and match. Some combinations will work together, and some won't. Keep a list of combinations in your logbook and record your satisfaction rating.

Knowing what works well this year and what does not work well will save time and money.

Over a few years, you will gather a comprehensive guide to companion planting in general, and specifically for your location.

Companion Plants

Plants for your Garden

All organic gardeners have learned that a diversified garden with a variety of different plants and trees makes for an attractive, healthy one. And I have to add that many experienced gardeners are of the firm belief that certain specific plant combinations even have mysterious, extraordinary powers to assist each other to grow to their full potential. Whether you agree with this or not, scientific studies of companion planting have confirmed the fact that certain combinations do have benefits that are exclusive to those specific combinations.

Lastly, many decades of practical experience in the field have taught gardeners just how to combine specific plants to the benefit of all of them.

Companion buddies assist each other in growing – taller plants will provide cooling shade for shorter, sun-sensitive ones. Its method of planting also makes efficient use of available garden space – while vining plants are covering the ground, the upright ones grow towards the sun so that two very different plants can grow happily in the same plot. Companions help with the prevention of all kinds of pests – strong-smelling plants like garlic and onion will repel insect pests. In contrast, others will lure these insects away from the more delicate seedlings and plants. Individual plants will even attract predators to prey on the pests which attack another plant.

Plants Which Should Always be Grown Together

Garlic and Roses

Seeing that garlic repels pests which attack roses, these two companions have long found themselves together in many gardens all over the world. If you prefer, you can try garlic chives; they are equally valid, and their tiny little white or purple flowers surely make a beautiful picture amongst the roses in spring.

Melons and Marigolds

Nematodes that can occur in the melon roots can be controlled by certain varieties of the marigold plant. Marigolds are maybe even more effective than chemical treatments against It pest.

Nasturtiums and Cucumbers

The vining stems of the nasturtium plant make it an excellent companion for the growing squash and cucumbers in their shared plot. Cucumber beetles are repelled by nasturtiums, and their rambling vines will make sure no beetle comes near your cucumbers. These same vines also make the perfect habitat for ground beetles, spiders and other predatory insects.

Pigweed and Peppers

A study was conducted at the Experimental Station in Coastal Plains in Georgia, which showed that leaf miners prefer ragweed and pigweed to pepper plants. You must remember, though, that you are dealing with a weed, so make sure you carefully remove all the flowers of the pigweed before the seeds setting or they will take over.

Dill and Cabbage

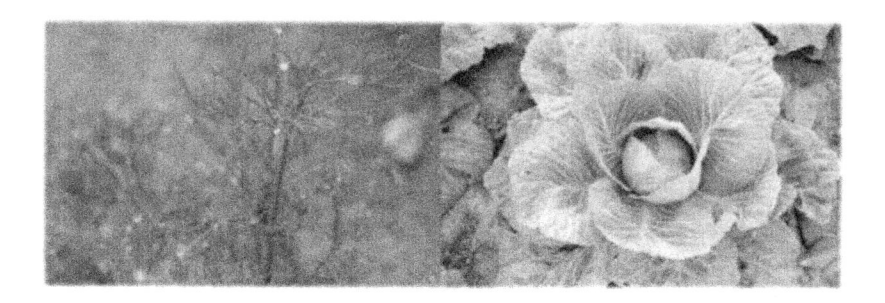

All the plants of the cabbage family like Brussels sprouts or broccoli are pleased to grow together with dill plants. While the floppy, drooping dill is supported by the cabbage, it, in turn, attracts those tiny little beneficial wasps which control cabbage worms and suchlike pests. (Just remember never to try to group dill and carrots).

Beans and Corn

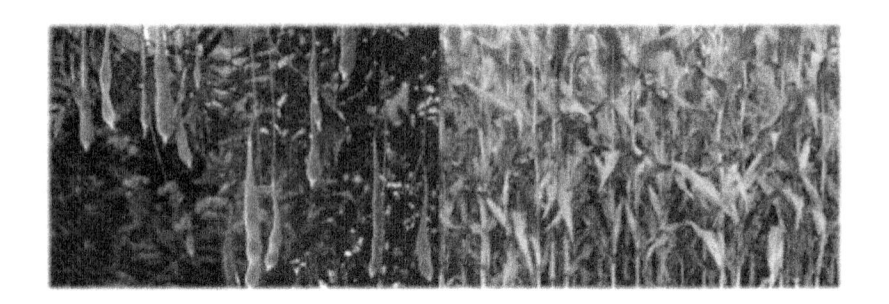

Firstly, bean vines planted to corn stalks have a natural pole against which their vines can climb up. Secondly, the beneficial predators that prey on insects like leaf beetles, leafhoppers and the fall armyworms which attack corn are attracted by the beans.

Tall Flowers and Lettuce

Lettuces like the shade, and this is what tall plants like the flowering tobacco or NICOTIANA, and the spider flower or cleome provide.

Spinach and Radishes

If you plant a few radishes amongst your spinach plants, they will draw the leaf miners to them instead of your precious spinach. You will still be able to harvest radishes since the damage they do is only to the leaves. At the same time, the bulbs continue to grow happily underground.

Sweet Alyssum and Potatoes

This border plant, which is actually (amongst the eighty or so that are even better than fences), with its tiny little flowers, attracts some delicate insects like predatory wasps beneficial to potatoes. Plant alyssum alongside any heavy crops, for example, potatoes. Otherwise, allow it to spread and cover the ground under your broccoli and other arching plants. There is a bonus to planting sweet alyssum; its lovely fragrance will fill your garden with its sweet scent right through the summer.

Dwarf Zinnias and Cauliflower

Beneficial predators like ladybugs are attracted by the nectar of the zinnias. These predators will keep pests away from your cauliflower plants.

Catnip and Collards

Catnip is one of only eight plants that naturally repel mosquitoes. They will also minimize the damage that can be caused by flea beetles to your collards.

Love-in-a-Mist and Strawberries

Beautify your garden by planting a few tall Nigella plants with their pretty blue flowers in the centers of your strawberry rows.

Plants which should never be planted together

The correct combination of plants grown together can be hugely beneficial. Still, also to inform you of those combinations, this should never be planted together. Individual pairs are simply natural enemies and make for unfriendly neighbors. The following is a list of the seven no-go combinations.

Peas and Onions

According to traditional wisdom, it is never a good idea to group peas together with any member belonging to the onion group, and that includes garlic and shallots. The Farmers' Almanac says that beans' and peas' growth will be stunted by the proximity of any onion variety.

Tomatoes and Potatoes

The problem with its combination is that they attract the very same blights. Planting those together means that you are providing a double attraction for the disease, and it will spread a lot easier.

Beans and Peppers

Both beans and peppers are susceptible to a disease called anthracnose, so if you plant them together, the disease will spread quickly from one to the other and destroy your entire crop. Soft dark spots appear on the fruits of the plants and ruin them.

Dill and Carrots

Gardeners all over believe that carrots and dill are fast enemies and should not be planted in combination. However, there are no scientific studies to substantiate this claim.

Grapes and Cabbage

According to folklore, planting your grapevines near your cabbage patch spells trouble; your home-grown grapes and homemade wine will not taste the same. Its unfavorable effect was already known amongst grape growers two thousand years ago, so I tend to believe it.

Tomatoes and Black Walnuts

These trees are quite infamous for being unfriendly neighbors to many a plant. The roots of the tree emit JUGLONE, a chemical toxic to any plants with deep roots, like tomatoes. If you have some of these walnut trees in your garden, you should consider growing your vegetables in raised beds or containers rather than in plots.

Broccoli and Lettuce

In scientific studies, it has been found that lettuce plants are quite sensitive to some of the chemicals left in the broccoli plant residue. I recommend you keep track of where you have grown broccoli before and never try to grow your crop of lettuce in the same spot as their growth and seed germinations could be hindered.

Soil Improvement

Soil groundwork for vegetable development includes a significant number of the standard tasks required for different yields. High seepage is particularly significant for raw vegetables since wet soil hinders advancement.

Sands are significant in developing fresh vegetables since they are more promptly depleted than the heavier soils. Soil seepage achieved by methods for trench or tiles is more alluring than the waste got by planting crops on edges because the abundant water as well as permits air to enter the dirt. Air is fundamental to the development of harvest plants and to particular useful soil creatures making supplements accessible to the plants.

At the point when yields are developed in progression, soil infrequently should be furrowed more than once every year. Furrowing consolidates grass, green-excrement harvests, and yield deposits in the dirt; crushes weeds and creepy crawlies; and improves soil surface and air circulation. Soils for vegetables ought to be genuinely profound. A profundity of six to eight inches (15 to 20 centimeters) is adequate in many soils.

Soil, the board, includes the activity of human judgment in the use of accessible information on crop creation, soil protection, and financial aspects. The executives ought to be coordinated toward delivering the ideal yields with at least work. Control of soil disintegration, support of natural soil issue, the selection of yield revolution, and clean culture are viewed as significant soil-the board rehearses.

Soil disintegration, brought about by water and wind, is an issue in numerous vegetable-developing locales because the topsoil usually is the most extravagant in ripeness and fundamental issue. Soil disintegration by water can be constrained by different techniques. Terracing isolates the land into discrete waste territories, with every territory having its conduit over the patio.

The patio holds the water on the land, permitting it to splash into the dirt and lessening or forestalling gullying. In the forming framework, crops are planted in lines at a similar level over the field. Development continues along with the columns as opposed to all over the slope. Strip trimming comprises of developing yields in restricted strips over an incline, generally on the shape. Soil disintegration by wind can be constrained by the utilization of windbreaks of different sorts, by keeping the dirt all around provided with humus, and by developing spread harvests to hold the dirt when the land isn't involved by different yields.

Support of the fundamental issue substance of the dirt is necessary. The fundamental issue is a wellspring of plant supplements. It is essential for its impact on specific properties of the dirt. Loss of natural issue is the aftereffect of the activity of miniaturized scale living beings that step by step disintegrates it into carbon dioxide. The expansion of excrements and the development of soil-improving harvests are effective methods for providing natural soil issues.

Soil-improving harvests are developed exclusively to set up the dirt for the development of succeeding yields. Green-fertilizer crops, developed mainly for soil improvement, are turned under while still green and ordinarily are developed during a similar period of the year as the vegetable harvests. Spread yields, raised for both soil insurance and improvement, are possibly developed during seasons when vegetable harvests don't possess the land. At the point when a speck of dirt improving harvest is turned under, the different supplements that have added to the development of the yield have come back to the dirt, including an amount of fundamental issue. The two vegetables, those plants, for example, peas and beans having products of the soil framed in pods, and non-legumes are viable soil-improving harvests.

The better the material is at the time it is turned under, the more rapidly it deteriorates. Since dry material breaks down more gradually than green material, it is alluring to turn under soil-improving harvests before they are full-grown, except if extended time is to slip by between the furrowing and the planting of the succeeding yield.

Plant material breaks down most quickly when the dirt is warm and all around provided with dampness. If dirt is dry when a speck of dirt improving harvest is turned under, almost no deterioration will happen until the downpour or water system supplies the critical dampness.

The central advantages gained from crop revolution are the control of sickness and creepy crawlies and the better utilization of the assets of the dirt. Turn is an orderly course of action for the developing of different yields in a pretty much customary succession on similar land.

It contrasts from progression editing in that pivot trimming covers a time of two, three, or more years, while in progression trimming at least two harvests are developed on similar land in one year. In numerous locales, vegetable harvests are developed in revolution with other ranch crops. Most vegetables developed as yearly harvests fit into a four-or five-year pivot plan.

The arrangement of intercropping, or buddy trimming, includes the development of at least two sorts of vegetables on similar land in a similar developing season. One of the vegetables must be a little developing and speedy developing harvest; the other must be bigger and late-developing.

In the act of clean culture, ordinarily followed in vegetable development, the dirt is kept liberated from all contending plants through continuous development and the utilization of defensive covers, or mulches, and weed executioners. In a spotless vegetable field, the chance of assault by bugs and infection INCITANT living beings, for which plant weeds fill in as hosts, is decreased.

Successful administration includes the selection of methods bringing about a consistent progression of the ideal measure of produce over the entire of the regular developing period of the yield. Many vegetables can be developed during the time in absolute atmospheres, even though the yield of land for a given sort of vegetable fluctuates as indicated by the developing season and district where the harvest is created.

1. Atmosphere:

The atmosphere includes the temperature, dampness, sunlight, and wind states of a particular locale. Climatic factors unequivocally influence all stages and procedures of plant development.

2. Temperature:

Temperature prerequisites depend on the base, ideal, and most extreme temperatures during both day and night all through the time of plant development. Prerequisites differ as indicated by the sort and assortment of the particular harvest. The ideal temperature ranges, vegetables might be classed as cool-season or warm-season types. Cool-season vegetables flourish in territories where the mean day by day temperature doesn't transcend 70° F (21° C).

3. Dampness:

The sum and yearly precipitation in a district, particularly during specific times of improvement, had influence neighborhood crops. Water-systems might be required to make up for lacking precipitation. For ideal development and improvement, plants require soil that provisions water just as supplements broke up in the water. Root development decides the degree of a plant's capacity to assimilate water and supplements. In dry soil, root development is incredibly hindered. Very wet soil additionally hinders root development by confining air circulation.

4. Sunlight:

Light is the wellspring of vitality for plants. The reaction of plants to light is reliant upon light force, quality, and every day, or photoperiod. The regular variety in day length influences the development and blooming of certain vegetable harvests. Continuation of vegetative development, as opposed to early blossom arrangement, is alluring in such harvests as spinach and lettuce.

At the point when planted exceptionally late in the spring, these harvests will, in general, produce blossoms and seeds during the long stretches of summer before they achieve adequate vegetative development to deliver the greatest yields. The base photoperiod required for the development of bulbs in garlic and onion plants varies among assortments, and nearby day length is a deciding component in the determination of assortments.

Certain blends may apply explicit impacts. Lettuce, for the most part, shapes a seed stalk during the long stretches of summer. Yet, the presence of blossoms might be deferred, or even forestalled, by moderately low temperature.

A horrible temperature joined with troublesome dampness conditions may cause the dropping of the buds, blossoms, and little products of the pepper, decreasing the harvest yield. Attractive territories for muskmelon creation are described by low moistness joined with high temperatures. In the creation of seeds of numerous sorts of vegetables, nonappearance of the downpour, or moderately light precipitation, and low dampness during aging, collecting, and relieving of the seeds are significant.

5. Site:

The decision of a site includes such factors as soil and climatic district. What's more, with the proceeded with the pattern toward specialization and automation, generally huge zones are required for business creation and sufficient water flexibly, and transportation offices are fundamental. Geography—that is, the outside of the dirt and its connection to different territories—impacts productivity of activity. In present-day automated cultivating, enormous, moderately level fields take into consideration lower working expenses.

Force hardware might be utilized to adjust geology. However, the expense of such land redesign might be restrictive. The measure of incline impacts the sort of culture conceivable. Fields with a moderate incline ought to form a procedure that may include included cost for the structure of porches and redirection trench. The bearing of a slant may impact the development time of yield or may bring about a dry spell, winter injury, or wind harm.

A level site is commonly generally attractive, albeit a slight slant may help seepage. Uncovered destinations are not reasonable for vegetable cultivating on account of the danger of harm to plants by solid breezes.

The dirt stores mineral supplements and water utilized by plants, just as lodging their foundations. There are two general sorts of soils—mineral and the natural kind called waste or peat. Mineral soils incorporate sandy, loamy, and clayey sorts. Sandy and loamy soils are typically favored for vegetable creation. Soil response and level of ripeness can be dictated by compound examination. The response of the dirt decides as it were, the accessibility of most plant supplements.

The level of corrosive, antacid, or nonpartisan response of dirt is communicated as the pH, with a pH of 7 being impartial, focuses beneath seven being corrosive, and those over seven being basic. The ideal pH extends for plant development differs, starting with one harvest. Dirt can be made progressively acid, or less antacid, by applying corrosive delivering synthetic manure, for example, ammonium sulfate.

Common Mistakes of Companion Planting

Salts

Excessive amounts of salt in your soil can directly affect your plants by damaging or even killing plant roots. Excessive salts can also indirectly affect your plant's health by absorbing water and reducing the amount of water available to plant roots.

Micronutrients

Many other nutrients are essential for healthy plant growth. The difference between these nutrients is the fact that these nutrients are only needed in very small amounts.

However, just because they are only needed in small amounts does not mean that they are not important. For example, a boron deficiency will prevent a plant from growing; a deficiency in iron and manganese will dramatically limit growth.

Because these nutrients are only needed in small amounts, they are referred to as micronutrients. Micronutrients include boron, copper, zinc, iron, manganese, selenium, cobalt, iodine, chromium and lithium. The good news is that it is very easy to ensure that all these vital micronutrients are available for your plants. Quality organic compost will fulfill all your plant's requirements for these micronutrients.

Not Testing your Soil

Do you know just how good your soil is? It might look good, it might feel good, but you have no other clue as to its quality. You need extra information. When you have this information, you can then start to provide an environment in which your plants will thrive. It is the first step you need to undertake.

What Does A Soil Test Reveal?

Your soil test will provide information particular to your soil only. Even within a small locale, the make-up of soil can vary greatly. When you see those wonderful healthy plants in other gardens a few miles down the road, you cannot assume that their soil is the same as yours. Testing your soil tells you what you need to add or subtract from your soil to make it the optimum growing environment for your plants.

Typically a soil test will reveal the following information about your soil.

1. PH

Determining the PH number of your soil will tell you if your soil is acidic or alkaline. It is very important because most plants grow best in soil that is neither too acidic nor too alkaline. They prefer soil that is neutral or only slightly acidic. PH is the scale used for this purpose. The scale ranges from 1.0 (acidic) to 14(alkaline). Ideally, you are looking to get your soil within the range of 6.0 (slightly acidic) to 7.0 (neutral).

A simple way of thinking about this is to think about pure, unadulterated water. Pure water is neutral, 7.0. Depending on what you add to the water, it will then become either more acidic or more alkaline. If you added vinegar to the water, it would become more acidic. If you added ammonia, it would become more alkaline.

Sample pH Scale

0-1 Battery Acid

1-2 Lemon Juice

2-3 Vinegar

3-4 Orange juice

4-5 Tomato juice and rain

5-6 Black coffee

6-7 Milk, urine

7 Pure water

8-9 Seawater

9-10 Baking sodas

10-11 Milk of magnesia

11-12 Ammonia Solution

12-13 Soapy water

13-14 bleach, drain cleaner.

The results of the PH test will reveal information.

2. Levels of Potassium and Phosphorus

Potassium (K)

Potassium is essential for healthy root development, disease resistance and fruit development. The most obvious sign of a potassium deficiency are stunted growth, older leaves look burned, and fruit does not fully develop.

Phosphorous (P)

Phosphorous deficiency results in very poor root growth and fruit development. Phosphorous is not as readily available within the soil as other nutrients, so plants with small root systems, as well as root crops, often struggle to access enough of it. Soils that are very sandy or exposed to strong winds will typically have very little organic matter. It lacks organic matter causes a deficiency of phosphorous.

3. Levels of Magnesium and Calcium

Magnesium (Mg)

Chlorophyll is the substance that gives plants their green color and helps them convert sunlight to energy.

Magnesium is a key part of chlorophyll, and a deficiency of Magnesium will mean that the process of converting that sunlight to energy is not working at its most efficient. When this happens, your plants will take their energy supplies from older leaves and send them to newer leaves. The obvious signs of It ailment are when your plant leaves start to dry up and fall off. A magnesium deficiency is a typical problem for acidic, sandy soils.

Calcium

Calcium is vital for the healthy development of plant cell walls. A calcium deficiency will result in very weak growth. Another physical sign of its presence is when your plant leaves start to curl-up and close.

4. Nitrogen

The nitrogen composition of your soil will have a dramatic impact on your plants. Its impact is even more obvious in fruiting plants. Not enough nitrogen will mean that your plants are slow to grow, and growth will be limited. Too much nitrogen will provide you with a lot of growth but not a lot of fruit.

Nitrogen levels in your soil can change from season to season, depending on the amount of organic matter within your soil. As organic matter breaks down, it releases nitrogen that plants can use. To achieve a productive level of nitrogen in your soil, you will need to ensure that you have a consistent level of organic matter in your soil. A generally accepted level of 5% of your soil should be organic matter. The physical signs of a nitrogen deficiency are plants with slow growth and pale leaves.

5. Sulfur (S) and Salts (Na)

Sulfur is essential for the formation of amino acids and proteins in plants. Sulfur is also required by nitrogen if it is to provide food for your plants effectively. All organic matter contains a large amount of sulfur, and this is another good reason for providing an ample amount of organic matter to your soil. Soil that is deficient in organic matter will be deficient in sulfur.

How to Take a Soil Sample

To provide the most accurate results, you will need to take 15 to 20 soil samples from the area you need to be tested. These samples will be mixed to provide a broader general picture of your soil condition. Simply repeat the process outlined below.

a. Get a large plastic bowl, spoon and small trowel or similar.

b. Scrape off loose debris from the top of the soil.

c. Insert spade to a depth of 6 to 8 inches and remove a spade full of soil. Place soil in a plastic bowl.

d. Now remove a few of soil from the side of the hole created by the spade. Place the removed soil in the bowl.

e. Repeat steps A to D until you have removed enough soil to give a good, general representation of your soil.

f. Mix all the collected soil. Remove roots, twigs Mix the soil until no clumps or solids remain. It is now your soil sample for testing.

Some private laboratories provide soil testing facilities, or you can use your local extension office. The following link will take you to a web page that provides both text and clickable links to all cooperative extension offices. As stated earlier, growing conditions can vary greatly from one local area to another.

When you have completed all the formalities, you should receive your results within 4 to 5 weeks.

These results will guide you as regards what to do. Commonly your results will be summarized as low, medium or high. There will be specific details regarding the nutrients described earlier, but in general terms, the following rules apply:

High = a soil that is rich in nutrients and does not need to be altered.

Medium = a soil that is currently nutrient-rich. Currently is the keyword. Everything is fine for the moment, but you will need to amend your soil in time for the following years' growing season.

Low = a soil that is severely lacking in nutrients. It is soil that needs to be amended immediately so that sufficient nutrients are available for your plants.

Excessive = It is a situation that many people fail to think. If your soil contains excessive levels of some nutrients, it will cause an imbalance. Remember, we are looking to get your soil as near to neutral as possible.

You will need to either add or remove certain nutrient sources to balance out and get nearer to neutral.

Perfect Combination

Some plants work best with each other, which is why they are considered "perfect combinations." Here are some of that you may want to try yourself.

- Cabbage and Tomatoes. Tomatoes can repel the Diamondback Moth larvae, which are infamous for chewing cabbage leaves and leaving large holes in them.

- Nasturtiums and Cucumbers. Cucumbers make use of Nasturtiums as trellises, while Nasturtiums can repel the dreaded cucumber beetles. They also serve as a natural habitat for ground beetles and spiders, which are predatory insects.

- Ragweed/Pigweed and Peppers. Ragweed and Pigweed are good weeds that can make the soil fertile and can protect plants from being infested by pests.

- Corn and Beans. Its combination has been used for thousands of years, and they are both able to attract beneficial insects such as leaf beetles and leaf horns. Aside from that, they also provide shade and trellis to each other, making sure that they both grow well and become beneficial for humans.

- Dill and Cabbage. They support each other in the sense that dill attracts wasps that eat pests and worms, making sure that the cabbages grow without holes.

- Chives and Roses. Garlic repels the pests that feed on roses, and they also look great when they are planted to each other.

- Tall Flowers and Lettuce. Tall flowers such as Cleomes and NICOTIANA give lettuce shade.

- Sweet Alyssum and Potatoes. Tiny flowers of sweet alyssum attract predatory wasps and also act as a shade for the potatoes.

- Catnip and Collard. They reduce beetle damage.

- Spinach and Radishes. They are both able to repel LEAFMINERS, and radishes can grow safe and well when planted with spinach.

- Dwarf Zinnias and Cauliflower. Dwarf Zinnias are great because their nectar lures predatory insects like ladybugs, and they are known to hunt down and eat common garden pests.

- Melons and Marigold. Marigold repels nematodes just as well as chemical treatments do.

- Love-in-a-mist and Strawberries. They are great for aesthetic purposes.

Here are a couple more companion plants that you can plant in your garden

- Anise. Anise is a good host for predatory wasps, which repels aphids and also camouflages the odor of the other plants to protect them from pests. Anise is best planted with Coriander or Cilantro.

- Amaranth. Amaranth is an annual plant that grows mostly in tropical conditions and is very beneficial when planted near sweet corn stalks. It acts as a shade for the corn, which can moisten the soil and allow corn to grow better and faster. Amaranth also plays host to ground beetles, which are predatory insects who feed on common pests.

- Bay Leaf. Bay leaf repels moths and weevils and can also act as a natural insecticide. Bay leaf is best planted with Tansy, Cayenne Pepper and Peppermint.

- Beets. Beets add minerals to the soil, especially nitrogen, which most plants need to grow. They are great fertilizers for the soil, too, as they contain 25% magnesium and are best planted with melon and corn.

- Bee Balm. When planted with tomatoes, bee balm can improve the growth and flavor of the tomatoes. Bee Balm also attracts bees and butterflies for pollination. She is also great for aesthetic purposes as it always looks good and fresh.

- Buckwheat. Buckwheat is a good cover crop as it is full of calcium and is also able to attract beneficial insects such as butterflies and bees, and repels pests such as aphids, flower bugs, pirate bugs and predatory wasps away. Buckwheat can also provide the soil with phosphorous in which other plants may also be able to benefit.

- Chards. Chards are good not only as vegetables but also as ornamental plants that make pollination possible by attracting beneficial insects. They are best planted with tomatoes, roses, beans, onions and cabbages.

- German Chamomile. It is an annual plant that can improve the flavor of cucumbers, cabbages and onions and also act as host to wasps and hoverflies. German Chamomile also gives soil protection by providing it with sulfur, potassium and calcium and also by increasing oil production in the herbs. Because of increased oil production, more people can benefit from their plants by making different kinds of aromatherapy oils.

- Clover. Clover works as a cover crop or green manure and is best planted near grapevines to attract beneficial insects and make pollination possible. When planted around apple trees, they can repel wooly aphids and also reduce cabbage aphids once planted near cabbages. Clover is also able to increase the number of ground beetles that are great for destroying non-beneficial insects.

- Castor Bean. Castor bean is a poisonous plant that is very effective in repelling moles and mice. And because it is poisonous, you need to be careful where you plant it.

- Chrysanthemums. Fondly called "mums," they can repel nematodes that destroy most plants easily. They are also used as botanical pesticides as they are full of Vitamin C that repels most pests, especially Japanese beetles. They work well with daisies in attracting beneficial insects in fertilizing your garden.

• Comfrey. An underrated plant, Comfrey, is beneficial because it gives calcium and potassium to the soil and also is a good medicinal plant. It also prevents foliage and is a good compost activator, as well as a nutrient miner. It is best planted with avocadoes.

• Costmary. Its flowering plant is very effective in the repulsion and killing of moths.

• Dahlia. While it looks harmless, the dahlia can repel nematodes.

• Four-o-clocks. These flowers can poison the dreaded Japanese beetles. Still, you also have to be careful because being around these flowers too much is also toxic to humans.

• Flax. Flax is used in most diets and is full of linseed oil and tannin that are very useful against the Colorado Potato Bug.

• Hemp. Hemp is very useful when planted near brassicas, as it can repel bugs and pests.

- Hyssop. Hyssop can repel cabbage moths and flea beetles and is best planted with grapes and cabbages. Hyssop is also able to attract bees, which are good for pollination. More often than not, bees make hyssops their homes, which is good for you as this means that your garden will be pollinated even more.

- Horehound. Horehound belongs to the Mint family and can attract beneficial insects such as ICHEUMONID and BRACONOID wasps that consume flies and other insects that feed on your plants.

- LAMIUM. Many gardeners and farmers think that LAMIUM is awesome because it can repel potato bugs which infest most plants and are not good for anyone's garden.

- Lavender. Lavender provides you with great essential oils and is also able to repel non-beneficial insects such as moths and fleas. It is also able to protect plants from whiteflies. Lavender is best planted during the winter season so it could bloom in spring.

- Larkspur. Larkspur can kill Japanese beetles, but you have to be careful around it as it is also poisonous to humans.

- Marjoram. Marjoram can improve the flavor of most fruits and vegetables and also attracts butterflies and bees so that pollination could happen. It's always best to grow sweet marjoram as it gives the best results.

- Morning Glory. Morning Glory attracts hoverflies and also makes the garden more beautiful as it is a vine.

- Stinging Nettles. These plants attract bees and are also full of calcium and silica that are essential for refreshing plants and improving resistance to diseases and also give the soil the nutrients it needs for plants to grow healthy and well.

- Okra. While it is not a vegetable favored by many, Okra is very useful as it gives shade to lettuce, especially during the summer season and prevents the lettuce from wilting. It is also able to protect eggplants and peppers from strong winds. It is also great when planted with peas, cucumber, basil and melons as it also repels aphids away.

- Opal Basil. Opal Basil grows annually and can repel hornworms. It is best planted with oregano, petunia, asparagus and peppers and must be kept away from sage and rue.

- Peach. Peach Trees give shade to asparagus, grapes, onions and garlic and may help repel tree borers and most other pests and insects.

- Hot Peppers. Hot peppers protect most plants' roots from being rotten and provide shelter for smaller plants, especially chili peppers and prevent other plants from being dried up or wilted. It is best planted with okra, green peppers and tomatoes.

- Pennyroyal a great plant that repels fleas, mosquitoes, gnats, flies and ticks.

- PURSLANE. It is a good cover crop for corn and makes the soil healthy and fertile.

- Rye. Prevents germs from targeting your plants and is great when planted near tomatoes and broccoli as well as with other vegetables.

- Soybeans. Soybeans provide nitrogen for the soil and also repel Japanese beetles and chinch bugs.

- Turnip. Turnip is also able to provide a lot of nitrogen to the soil and is best planted with peas and cabbage. Do not plant near potatoes, though, as turnip stunts their growth.

• White Geraniums. White Geraniums are effective in repelling Japanese beetles.

The Importance of Compost for Soil Quality

Soil quality plays a massive role in the overall health of your garden. No other single factor is as important. If you have any doubts over the quality of your soil or if you want to stay chemical-free, you need to use compost. Quality compost will provide all the nutrients required for healthy plants. When combined with companion planting, it is the perfect relationship.

Compost improves the condition of soil through altering its biological, physical and chemical properties. Some of the most obvious ways in which compost improves soil conditioning are as follows.

1. It improves soil structure in clay type soil. It improved soil structure results in the clay type soil becoming firmer, more distinct and less prone to clotting. In turn, it leads to better drainage, more nutrients, more aeration and, ultimately, better-growing conditions.

2. It improves the water retention ability of sandy soil by providing a medium in which water can be retained. It results in less rapid loss of water and a more consistent source of liquid for plants. It means that sandy soils are still suitable for plants that do not like to have their roots in water for prolonged periods but that they also have access to water, thus avoiding drought.

3. Compost improves the fertility levels of soil, which in turn means that they need to use chemical fertilizers is greatly reduced or, in some cases, totally removed.

4. Composting your soil increases microbial activity within the soil, which leads to increased resistance to foliar and soil-borne diseases.

5. The increased microbial activity caused by the addition of compost also results in increased efficiency in breaking down pesticides and similar compounds.

6. The addition of compost also reduces the bioavailability of dangerous heavy metals. It is a significant issue when contaminated soils are being reclaimed as healthy soils.

Under normal conditions, organic matter would be broken into small pieces by an army of earthworms, mites, ants, beetles. The resulting organic material would then be further broken down by the presence of fungi, bacterial and protozoa. These microorganisms require certain temperatures to perform optimally.

When we create a compost pile, we are attempting to provide the ideal conditions for the breakdown of organic matter. We do this by providing the following basic components.

1. Organic matter.

2. Minerals.

3. Water.

4. Microorganisms.

5. Oxygen

When all these 'raw materials' come together under certain conditions, we get compost. To make the process even more efficient and faster, we follow certain rules. When these rules are applied consistently, the result is higher quality compost produced faster than if left to run its natural course of events.

Essential Compost Ingredients

The essential ingredients for quality compost are as listed:

1. Organic matter.

2. Minerals.

3. Water.

4. Microorganisms.

5. Oxygen.

However, providing these ingredients alone will not provide you with quality compost. There is a specific recipe that needs to be followed. Like all good recipes, the result is entirely dependent on using the correct quantities of the correct ingredients correctly. All of the ingredients provided above will determine three important factors.

1. The feedstock. It is the chemical makeup of the raw organic ingredients.

2. The actual physical and shape and size of the feedstock.

3. The population of the microorganisms that is vital to the process.

The Composting Recipe

Bacteria, fungi, microbes, worms and other invertebrates are the workers of the compost pile. It is their work that produces the nutrient-rich compost that plants love. These are the decomposers. Their job is to break down all the materials that we put in the compost pile.

As with any workers, they need to be well-fed. Each one has a preferred diet, and when they all have what they need, the compost pile is working at its most efficient. The trick to making great compost is to provide the ideal conditions for all those decomposer workers to thrive.

Most materials we use in a pile are not ideal for these decomposers. They need a good balance of Carbon (C) and Nitrogen (N) to be efficient. Carbon gives them the energy they need, and Nitrogen gives them the protein they need. Ideally, they prefer a ratio of Carbon to Nitrogen at a rate of 30C: 1N

To give them It ratio and thereby have a healthy compost pile, we need to pay attention to the materials we are using in a pile. The best way to do this is to think of Greens and Browns.

Greens = Nitrogen = Food Scraps, Grass Clippings, Vegetables, Fruit and extensive garden, clear out.

Browns = Carbon = Brown Leaves, Straw, Woodchip, Saw Dust, Newspapers

Maintaining a balance between Greens and Browns also helps with the structural stability of the pile since many of the Green ingredients will be moist or wet, and much of the Brown ingredients will be dry. The Green ingredients do provide necessary moisture content, and the Green helps to prevent the pile from becoming too compacted. Again it is a balance, but It time between moisture retention and air-flow.

Achieving all of the above leaves us with a balance between moisture, air, the carbon and nitrogen provided by the raw materials and the agents of decomposition, i.e., bacteria, insects, fungi, worms, will finish the process.

How is A Compost Pile Layered?

A properly structured and well-managed compost pile can be ready for use within four months in warm temperatures. The structure of the pile is very important, you already know the right ingredients to use, and it is now time to layer them correctly.

The basic structure of a compost pile from bottom to top is a series of layers that begin on a hard surface. You can start your pile on top of pallets, but starting it on a hard surface such as concrete or compacted soil means easier turning. However, using concrete makes it more difficult for beneficial organisms and worms to reach the soil.

My personal preference is to use a suitably sized area and clear it of all grass I then lightly aerate the soil with my fork. It is the best of both worlds. It provides a solid surface that allows you to turn the compost. Still, it allows for quick establishment of contact between worms and the compost pile. Once you have your base ready, it is then time to start building your pile.

Step 1: Place a base layer of materials that will provide carbon like shredded newspapers, dead leaves, wood chips, small twigs and branches. Make them no bigger than 2 to 3 inches in size. Smaller sized materials and greater surface area exposure will speed up the decomposition process. If you have enough materials, you should aim to make this first layer 4 to 6 inches deep. When It layer is in place, you should lightly moisten it.

Step 2: Start your second layer. Its layer consists of nitrogen-rich materials such as grass clippings, fruit and vegetable waste, eggshell, coffee grounds, leftover bread and rice and leafy garden trimmings. If you have access to seaweed, you should use it. Seaweed is an excellent addition to a compost pile. Its layer of nitrogen materials should be 2 to 3 inches deep.

Step 3: You will notice that the first layer of carbon-rich materials was 4 to 6 inches deep and that the second layer of nitrogen-rich materials was 2 to 3 inches deep. It is your ratio guide of approximately two parts carbon to 1 part nitrogen. Try to maintain that approximate ratio by using the thickness of the layers as a guide, i.e., 4 to 6 inches for carbon 2 to 3 inches for nitrogen. Now repeat the process as described in steps 1 and 2.

Step 4: After repeating these layers, your compost pile should now be reaching 4 to 5 feet in height. If you are using a bin, it is time to close it, and if you are using an open compost pile, you should now cover it with plastic.

Step 5: Start a new compost pile using steps 1 to 4.

Step 6: You will need to monitor the moisture content of the pile. Use this sponge test, soak a sponge in water and then squeeze the water out, the moisture content of a wrung-out sponge is approximately the moisture content you are looking for with your compost. You need it moist, not soaking wet. Squeeze a few handfuls of the compost. Ideally, it should yield a few drops of liquid.

If the compost is too wet, grab your fork and turn the compost over. It will allow air in around the compost as well as improve drainage.

If the compost is very dry, you simply need to water it, turn it and water it again. Use the test described earlier to ensure that you do not overwater.

Step 7: Temperature plays a large role in the decomposition process. You will need to check the internal temperature of your compost pile occasionally. You can use your hands or purchase a compost thermometer.

If using your hands, the compost should be hot to touch. If using a thermometer, it should be within the range of 120 to 160.

Check every 2 to 3 weeks. When the temperature starts to decrease, it is time to turn the compost.

Step 8: To turn the compost, you simply need to move the materials from the outside and the top of the compost into the middle and move the middle materials to the outside and top.

It is an easy process if you have a second composting area nearby and ready to go. If not, all you need to do is to grab your fork and dig towards the center of the pile. As you dig, place what you have just removed in a small pile to the side. When you have a significant hole dug into the pile, you just need to start filling the hole with material from the outside of the pile.

When the center is now filled up again, spread the compost you set aside along the top and outer parts of the pile. Inside out, outside in!

Step 9: Wait a few weeks and check the inner temperature again. You are looking for 'hot to touch' or 120 to 160. When your pile reaches this temperature, it will need to be turned one final time.

Step 10: Its stage, you have turned your pile twice, and it is unlikely to heat to those temperatures again. It should start to cool down, so now it is a waiting game. Wait for it to cool down and then give it another 3 to 4 weeks. Timings may vary, but that is the general period involved.

Step 11: Your compost should now be ready to use. It will be a lot smaller than it was originally and will be crumbly in texture. There should not be any significant odor.

Good and Bad Companion

Good Companions

Here is a list of plants that grow well together, with a brief explanation of just why this is the case. Although It list is not by any means an exhaustive list in itself; it only takes a little imagination to bring different species together, when you have the most basic gardening skills. The knowledge that is contained in these notes to guide you.

Asparagus:

Best companions include: Tomato, parsley and Basil; and French marigold planted alongside will deter beetles. If on its own or just with Tomato plants, then Comfrey can be planted around as a good source of nitrogen for both plants.

Beans:

Companions include; Beetroot, cabbage, celery, carrot, cucumber, corn, squash, pea's, potatoes, radish, strawberry.

Beans produce (draw from the air) nitrogen that is beneficial to the other plants

Nasturtium and rosemary can deter bean Beatles, while Marigolds can deter Mexican bean Beatles.

Cabbage Family:

Companions include; cucumber, lettuce, potato, onion, spinach, celery.

Chamomile and garlic can be grown to improve growth and flavor.

Marigolds and Nasturtium can be grown alongside to act as a decoy for butterflies and aphid pests. While mint, rosemary and sage will also deter cabbage moth and ants – as well as improve flavor.

Marigolds planted to carrots attract hoverflies, whose larvae, in turn, eat aphids. The smell of the marigold flowers also confuse the carrot fly

Carrots:

Good companions include beans, peas, onions, lettuce, tomato, and radish.

Including chives in the area will improve flavor and growth. At the same time, onions or leeks will distract the carrot fly by masking the scent of the carrots, as will sage or rosemary.

Celery:

Bean, tomato and cabbage family make good companions for celery.

Nasturtium, chives and garlic deter aphids and other bugs.

Corn:

Good companions are Potato, pumpkin, squash, tomato and cucumber.

French marigold deters beetles and attracts aphids from tomatoes.

Cucumber:

Good companions include cabbage, beans, cucumber, radish, tomato.

Marigold and Nasturtium are good for attracting to themselves, aphids and beetles. Oregano is a good all-round pest deterrent.

Lettuce:

Cabbage, carrot, beet, onion, and strawberry are all good companions for Lettuce.

Chives and garlic discourage aphids.

Melon:

Companions include pumpkin, radish, corn, and squash.

Marigold and Nasturtium deter bugs and beetles as oregano.

Onions:

Good Companions include the cabbage family, beet, tomato, pepper, strawberry, peas, and chard.

Chamomile and summer savory helps improve growth and flavor. Pigweed brings up nutrients from the subsoil and improves conditions for the onions.

Parsley:

Good companions include asparagus, tomato and corn.

Peas:

Good companions include beans, carrot, corn and radish.

Chives and onions help deter aphids as nasturtium.

Planting mint is known to improve the health and flavor of peas.

Peppers:

Tomato, eggplant, carrot and onion are known to be good companions for peppers.

Potatoes:

Good companions include bean, cabbage, squash and peas.

Marigold makes a good general deterrent for beetles, while horseradish planted around the potato patch gives good overall insect protection.

Pumpkin:

Melon eggplant and corn make good companions for pumpkin.

Oregano and Marigold give good all-round insect protection.

Radish:

Companions are carrot, cucumber, bean, pea, melon.

Nasturtium planted around is generally accepted to improve growth and flavor.

Squash:

Companions include melon, pumpkin, squash and tomato, while nasturtium and marigold, along with oregano, helps protect against bugs and beetles.

Strawberry:

Good companions include bean, lettuce, onion and spinach.

Planting thyme around the border deters worms, while borage strengthens general resistance to disease.

Tomatoes:

Good companion plants for tomatoes include; celery, cucumber, asparagus, parsley, pepper and carrot.

Basil and dwarf marigold deter flies and aphids; mint can improve health and all-around flavor.

These are some examples from popular vegetable types and offer a guide as to what to consider for your companion garden.

Bad Companions

There are a few reasons why some plants should not be grown alongside others if you are considering the organic method of growing your vegetables.

I mention particularly organic because the general idea behind companion planting is to avoid the use of chemical pesticides and fertilizers whenever possible.

Some plants should not be grown together simply because they both attract the same pests or other predators, others because they make the same demands on the soil, leading to them both producing a poor harvest. Some plants grown close together may produce a damp environment that leads to fungal or other infections.

Here are some plants to avoid planting close together, if possible, when considering a companion for your veggies.

Beans:

Beans should not be grown in the same vicinity of garlic, shallot or onions as they tend to stunt the growth.

Beets:

Beets should not be grown along with pole beans as they stunt each other's growth.

Cabbage

It is generally thought not to do well near tomatoes, mainly because the tomato plant can shade the cabbage. Avoid planting near radishes, as they do not grow well together.

Carrots:

Avoid planting near dill as this can stunt growth. Dill and carrots both belong in the UMBELLIFERAE family. If allowed to flower, it will cross-pollinate with the carrots.

Avoid planting alongside Celery as this is from the same family.

Corn:

Where possible, avoid planting corn and tomatoes together, as they both attract the same tomato fruit-worm.

Cucumber:

Sage should be avoided near cucumber, as it is generally harmful to the cucumber plant.

Peas:

Onions and garlic stunt the growth of peas.

Potatoes:

Tomatoes and potatoes should not be planted together as they attract the same blight, and use up the same nutrients from the soil.

Radish:

Avoid planting hyssop near radishes.

Make Your Special Mix for Infilling Compost

These are altogether obvious if you manure the incorrect way. Fertilizing the soil the correct way is a straightforward methodology: Simply layer organic materials and a scramble of soil to make a blend that transforms into humus (the best soil manufacturer around!). You would then be able to improve your blossom garden with fertilizer, top dress your grass, feed your developing veggies, and the sky is the limit from there. With these straightforward strides on the most proficient method to compost, you'll have the entirety of the boasting privileges of a star!

Fertilizer

Kinds of Composting

Before you begin heaping on, perceive that there are two kinds of treating the soil: cold and hot. Cold treating the soil is as straightforward as gathering yard waste or taking out the organic materials in your garbage, (for example, foods grown from the ground strips, espresso beans and channels, and eggshells) and afterward corralling them in a heap or canister. Through the span of a year or thereabouts, the material will break down.

Sweltering fertilizing the soil is for the more genuine nursery worker; however, a quicker procedure—you'll get fertilizer in one to a quarter of a year during warm climate. Four fixings are required for quick-cooking hot manure: nitrogen, carbon, air, and water. Together, these things feed microorganisms, which accelerate the procedure of rot. In spring or fall, when nursery squander is plentiful, you can blend one major clump of manure and afterward start a subsequent one while the primary "cooks."

Vermicomposting is made utilizing worm treating the soil. At the point when worms eat your nourishment scraps, they discharge castings, which are wealthy in nitrogen. You can't utilize only any old worms for this, be that as it may—you need REDWORMS (likewise called "red wigglers"). Worms for treating the soil can be bought reasonably on the web or at a nursery provider.

What to Compost

Fertilizing the soil is an incredible method to utilize the things in your cooler that you didn't get to, consequently wiping out waste. Keeping a holder in your kitchen, similar to Its chic white earthenware manure can from World Market, is a simple method to aggregate you're fertilizing the soil materials. If you would prefer not to get one, you can make your own indoor or open-air handcrafted fertilizer container. Gather these materials to begin your manure heap right:

- Organic product scraps

- Vegetable pieces

- Espresso beans

- Eggshells

- Grass and plant clippings

- Destroyed paper

- Straw

- Sawdust from untreated wood

What NOT to Compost

Not exclusively will these things not fill in also in your nursery. However, they can make your fertilizer smell and pull in creatures and vermin. Stay away from these things for an effective manure heap:

- Sick plant materials

- Sawdust or chips from pressure-treated wood

- Pooch or feline defecation

- Weeds that go to seed

- Dairy items

- Manure, grass clippings, leaves

Stage 1: Combine Green and Brown Materials

To make your hot-fertilizer store, hold up until you have enough materials to make a heap at any rate 3 feet down. You are going to need to consolidate your wet, green things with your dry, earthy colored things. "Earthy colored" materials incorporate dried plant materials; fallen leaves; destroyed tree limbs, cardboard, or paper; roughage or straw; and wood shavings, which include carbon. "Green" materials incorporate kitchen scraps and espresso beans, creature excrements (not from pooches or felines), and new plant and grass trimmings, which include nitrogen. For best outcomes, begin fabricating your manure heap by blending three earthy colored with one green material. If your fertilizer heap looks excessively wet and scents, include increasingly earthy colored things or circulate air through more frequently. If you see, it looks very earthy colored and dry, add green things and water to make it somewhat soggy.

Stage 2: Stir Up Your Pile

During the developing season, you ought to furnish the heap with oxygen by turning it once every week with a nursery fork. The best time to turn the manure is the point at which the focal point of the heap feels warm or when a thermometer peruses somewhere in the range of 130 and 150 degrees F. Working up the heap will assist it with cooking quicker and keeps material from getting tangled down and building up a smell. Now, the layers have filled their need to make equivalent measures of green and earthy colored materials all through the heap, so mix all together.

Stage 3: Feeding the Garden

At the point when the fertilizer no longer radiates heat and gets dry, earthy colored, and brittle, it's completely cooked and prepared to take care of to the nursery. Add around 4 to 6 crawls of fertilizer to your bloom beds and into your pots toward the start of each planting season.

Stage 4: Watering the Pile

Try not to include an excessive amount of water; in any case, the microorganisms in your heap will get waterlogged and suffocate. If this occurs, your heap will decay rather than a fertilizer. Screen the temperature of your heap with a thermometer to be certain the materials are appropriately disintegrating. Or, on the other hand, essentially venture into the center of the heap with your hand. Your manure heap should feel warm.

A few gardeners make what's known as manure tea with a portion of their completed fertilizer. It includes permitting full-grown manure to "steep" in water for a few days, then stressing it to use as handcrafted fluid compost.

Each planter is different, so it's dependent upon you to choose which treating the soil strategy best accommodates your lifestyle. Luckily, regardless of which course you pick, fertilizer is extraordinarily simple and naturally cordial. Besides, it's a treat for your nursery. With only a couple of kitchen scraps and some tolerance, you'll have the most joyful nursery conceivable.

How to Grow Healthy Organic Herbs

Herbs are such an awesome blessing from the unstoppable force of life from various perspectives. Their utilizations are many, including culinary, therapeutic, family unit, restorative, and art. Also, their utilizations in the garden as companion plants and many can be utilized as activators in the fertilizer load.

Also, there's no better method to thoroughly enjoy their sharp fragrant characteristics than to grow them directly outside your kitchen entryway.

When you have an herb garden, you will experience passionate feelings for them. Most herbs are genuinely simple to grow. They don't need to occupy a lot of room, Thyme or quite a bit of your time.

Herbs don't experience the ill effects of insects' assault, and they are not inclined to infection issues. Most will endure regardless of whether very dismissed. However, we need our herbs to grow solid and vivaciously to serve us best. So, we should take a look at making the best conditions for your herb garden.

Where to Grow Your Herbs

If you are sufficiently fortunate to have a lot of space for a plot committed to growing herbs, at that point, that is great, a creative and pragmatic approach to grow herbs together is in a winding. I like to interplant herbs all through my garden, exploiting their excellent Companion Planting benefits, just as having the ones I utilize most in the kitchen close by for simple access.

Numerous herbs start from the Mediterranean and incline toward conditions fit to that atmosphere. For example, hot, dry summers and cold, wet winters. Frequently the hotter the summer, the more fragrant the oils of the herb become.

Albeit most herbs will grow in halfway shade, they will grow best if you choose a site with somewhere in the range of 4 and 6 hours of daylight for every day.

Most of the herbs lean toward an all-around depleted soil; however, they will adapt to shifting soil types. You can generally improve your starting soil by including fundamental issues, including manure and mulching. If your soil doesn't deplete well, you should seriously think about structure raised beds or growing your herbs in containers.

Most herbs don't require much in the method for composts. Including fertilizer as mulch with a layer of pea straw or comparative over the top is sufficient to keep most herbs flourishing.

Growing Your Herbs in Containers

Herbs are probably the most straightforward plants to grow in containers. With some idea to the position of the sun, you can grow them effectively on porches, overhangs, patios, and verandas. Along these lines, you can have them at your indirect access – or even in your window ledge.

Container growing is especially helpful if you live in a freezing winter atmosphere, with the goal that you can over-winter your herbs in containers inside.

It's likewise a great method to grow a portion of the herbs you regularly use in case you're leasing. At the point when you leave, you simply take your herb containers with you!

You can choose practically any container to grow herbs in. You could get very creative with your box as long as it has enough seepage and isn't something that may have any dangerous buildup. However, in case you're not too creative, there are custom planters, enormous shallow pots that permit a few types of herbs to grow together, strawberry pots, and window boxes – and I'm sure there are a lot more alternatives.

Littler herbs will be the best decision for container plants. You may be astonished at what number of types of herbs would be upbeat growing together in a similar pot.

Picking moderate growing herbs will imply that you won't need to keep them clean. Clipping what you need for supper will keep them minimized and shaggy. Continuously select sound herbs to give them the best start. Expel any dead or infected leaves to keep them solid.

While preparing them up into their container, recall that they'll be there for some time, so choose a decent, very much depleted preparing mix. Since most herbs don't require a great deal of compost, choose a preparing mix without included manure. Container plants require more thoughtfulness regarding watering needs as they will dry out a lot quicker than plants in the ground. On hot, dry days, you may need to water little containers two times every day.

Occasional Care

Keeping gets rid of your herb garden and watering great during summer are the two fundamental necessities to keeping your set up herbs solid. Mulching will be major assistance with both of these assignments. It will likewise help keep your herb roots cool. Apply a thick layer of mulch – around 3 or 4 inches/8-10 cm to be successful. If you live in a zone with severe winters, you should over-winter a few herbs or treat them as annuals and plant new plants in spring.

Brilliant Oregano

If a portion of your herb plants starts to get, "leggy" trim them practically back to ground level toward the finish of summer. Herbs that will profit by this include oregano, marjoram, all the mints, yarrow, lemon medicine.

A portion of the more bush-like herbs simply needs cutting back to energize rugged growth, for example, rosemary, lemon verbena, and lavender.

What's more, a few herbs ought to be treated as annuals – as such, force them up after the primary growing season and plant new plants growing season. It incorporates basil, dill, chervil, borage, coriander, cumin.

You will profit greatly by remembering herbs for your natural garden. They offer such a lot yet ask pretty much nothing.

A few herbs are best treated as groundcovers; some make superb edging plants; however, I want to grow the majority of my herbs among different plants. They make their mark when their excellence and fragrances can be experienced personally and frequently.

Conclusion

Thank you for making it to the end of Companion Planting, you can enjoy the benefits of companion planting to make your garden healthier and more productive, and without having to work as hard to repel pests or keep your crops robust. Starting with a solid foundation of healthy soil that is rich in organic matter, carefully plan out how to arrange your companion garden to get the most out of your space.

Remember that increasing yield is not just about spatial efficiency, but also about extending the growing season to be as long as possible. By applying the principles of companion planting, you can have a beautiful, productive garden that takes care of itself. Companion planting is an important way to shift to using more sustainable, organic methods of keeping your garden healthy.

The key to successful companion planting is properly planning where the plants in your garden are going to go. You've got to carefully consider how each of the plants in your garden is going to interact with one another and then place them in the best possible locations to take advantage of those interactions. The biggest limitation regarding companion planting is the knowledge of the gardener. Arm yourself with as much knowledge as possible before you ever put on your gardening gloves.

Keep in mind that one of the most common mistakes that you should never attempt to do is to start big with companion gardening. Even if you have a big lawn or backyard intended for this purpose, you should always try a smaller plot first.

Assess your budget and how much time you want to commit to getting the garden started, and base your decision on that. To maintain a companion garden, you don't need too many materials. A source of water is, of course, essential, whether it is a rain barrel, well pump, or spout. Beyond that, a sturdy spade, a garden rake or hoe, and a trowel are all you need.

Remember that in Companion planting, there are millions of types of insects. Still, not all of them are pests determined to devour your crops. There are a lot of species which are referred to under the umbrella term of 'beneficial insects,' which provide a natural form of pest control. For many gardeners, including myself, they are an essential part of organic and natural gardening.

Once you know which plants you want to grow and what your primary goals for companion planting are, it's time to get your system into action. It book will explain how to get started with companion planting in the real world – taking your plans and making them a reality in your garden.

By weaning your garden off of chemical fertilizers and insecticides, and using natural methods to keep your plants healthy and free of pests, you will be improving not only your plants' health but your own as well. You'll also be improving the environmental and carbon footprints. And your garden will be more robust as a result and better equipped to handle various weather conditions, droughts, and disease. Good luck!

Printed in Great Britain
by Amazon